This book is dedicated to all who cherish America's history as a vast heritage of people and events — some heroic, some inglorious, but all part of America's epic struggle to come of age — and to all who know that understanding the past is essential to dealing with the present.

COLONIAL
NATIONAL HISTORICAL PARK
THE STORY BEHIND THE SCENERY®

By James N. Haskett

James N. Haskett is the Chief of Interpretation of Colonial National Historical Park. Jim has spent over 34 years in the historical areas of the National Park Service. The challenge of both preserving and interpreting the unique resources of each park has made every assignment a special experience.

Colonial National Historical Park, *located in southeastern Virginia, was authorized in 1930 to preserve the first permanent English settlement in the New World and the site of the American Revolution's last major battle.*

Front cover: Colonists coming ashore. NPS—Artist: Sidney King. Inside front cover: Cannon at Colonial National Historical Park Visitor Center, photo by Russ Finley. Title page: "One Country," photo by Jeff Gnass. Pages 2/3: Surrender Field at Yorktown, photo by Jeff Gnass.

Edited by Mary L. Van Camp and Russell D. Butcher • Book design by K. C. DenDooven

Second Printing, 1992
COLONIAL NATIONAL HISTORICAL PARK: THE STORY BEHIND THE SCENERY © 1990 KC PUBLICATIONS, INC.
LC 90-60042 ISBN 0-88714-044-0

*S*ilent today, this field witnessed not only the close of the Yorktown campaign, but also the end of the British dream of empire in today's United States. This dream had its beginnings at Jamestown, only twenty miles away. Colonial National Historical Park chronicles this story.

NPS—ARTIST: SIDNEY KING

Colonial National Historical Park—selecting this name for the park was a bold decision, confusing to some, considering that five nations sought to establish colonies in America. However, English colonists certainly made the greatest impact on the birth and growth of this nation. The park unquestionably represents a concentration of related English Colonial sites that has no equal either in scope or significance elsewhere in the United States.

Eastern Virginia is called "Tidewater" because the rivers move to the rhythm of the ocean before they finally merge with Chesapeake Bay. The area between the James and York rivers is known simply as "the Peninsula," and it is here that our story unfolds.

The mouth of the James River aligns directly with the entrance to Chesapeake Bay from the Atlantic Ocean. As Virginia's longest river, the James enabled the early settlers to explore far inland in search of the fabled passage to the wealth of China. Exploration led to settlement, and so the lands along the James River were the first to be colonized.

While the entire Peninsula is rich in history, one section stands above all others in importance.

The *Historic Triangle* (also called the *Triple Shrines*), encompasses three major historical areas: Jamestown—site of the initial landing and first century of settlement; Williamsburg—18th-century capital and scene of many events that contributed to the beginning of the American Revolution; Yorktown—where a crucial military victory made national independence possible.

This extraordinary coincidence received little permanent recognition until the establishment of Colonial National Monument in 1930—redesignated Colonial National Historical Park in 1936. The park presents a unique chapter in this nation's park preservation movement. It was the first strictly historical area staffed within the national park system, and provided the prototype for the hundreds of other historical areas subsequently added to the system.

This park, along with the Colonial Williamsburg restoration, created earlier, provided a well-deserved and permanent recognition by the nation of the significance of the Historic Triangle.

The American Colonial Experience

The English colonists arrived in the New World determined to secure Virginia for themselves and for England. This area was already inhabited by a large and culturally advanced population of Native Americans. It was home to an Algonquian-speaking confederation of some 32 tribes ruled by Powhatan. Accounts seemed to differ as to his title (great werowance or chief), but no one questioned that he was in control.

Although the world of the 17th-century Virginia Indian may have seemed relatively stable, it was far from idyllic. Constant warfare between the tribes was a fact of life. Food supplies, while normally bountiful, were not dependable. With a hard winter, a drought, a hurricane, or a plague, all would go hungry and some would die. It is understandable that during such periods the Indi-

ED COOPER

ans were reluctant to share their limited food supply with the English settlers.

While the colonists knew little of the natives, there is evidence that the reverse was not true. The Indians' unprovoked attack, when the settlers first landed at Cape Henry, would indicate some past unpleasant experiences with Europeans.

Although many Englishmen regarded them as little more than a barrier to progress, the colonists' survival in this often hostile environment would have been difficult if not impossible without many skills learned from the Indians.

It was inevitable that the Europeans, with their vast numbers and superior technology, would prevail. Native Americans, whose very survival required large amounts of land and care to preserve the balance of nature, tried alternately to coexist with or repel the invaders. Neither attempt proved successful, and by the end of the 17th century the Indian had virtually vanished from the Tidewater.

TWO CULTURES MEET

In May 1607, the *Susan Constant*, the *Godspeed*, and the *Discovery* anchored off a low-lying marshy island which their English passengers called Jamestown in honor of King James I. Soon the ships sailed back to England, leaving 104 men and boys alone to conquer the wilderness.

Who were these first settlers and those who soon followed them? The first few waves of settlers were composed of many aristocratic individuals who saw Virginia as a chance to get rich and return to England with enough wealth to live

The first of many tests for the would-be Virginia settlers was the sea voyage. These tiny ships provided cramped quarters, often spoiled food, foul water, and frequently disease for the adventurers. All too often the newcomers arrived badly weakened to face the rigors of this new land and life.

the good life. After all, wasn't that what the Spaniards had done in Central and South America?

These new colonists came from all walks of life. During the initial settlement period a number of them were identified as gentlemen, who by definition were those who did no physical work. These aristocrats, as well as jewelers, tailors, and persons of similar professions, were not well suited to survive in or contribute to life in this often unforgiving environment.

The developers of the colony ultimately learned their lesson through bitter experience. In time, settlers were recruited almost entirely from the ranks of the working class. Carpenters, masons, and other skilled craftsmen as well as unskilled laborers were quickly absorbed into the almost never-ending task of taming a wilderness.

The British survived by learning from the Indians how to coexist in this often unforgiving environment. The Indians would save the colonists from starvation at times, only to prove deadly enemies at others. They first regarded the newcomers as potential allies and too late recognized them as a grave danger to their way of life.

Whatever their background, those who risked all to come to Virginia did so from either an urgent need to leave England or for the promise that America held for those who wanted a better life.

Although the colonists sought to leave England, they did not wish to cease being English. In Virginia they strove to duplicate and adhere to the familiar customs and way of life of their homeland. Basic institutions were occasionally altered

Many of the first settlers were ill equipped to deal with their new life. Coming from cities or parts of England far different than Virginia, they had to learn to either do for themselves or do without. Untrained craftsmen working with unfamiliar materials created homes that were not always comfortable or permanent.

LINDA GALLO FETZER

to respond to needs in an untamed land, but they would remain essentially unchanged throughout the entire Colonial period.

These early settlers were not against the system, they only wanted to reap the benefits of that system. Their strong attachment to the basic rights and privileges of an Englishman would never waiver. It is ironic that at this very time many of these same basic rights and privileges were being strongly contested in England between the king and Parliament.

THE DEADLY PRICE OF THE GAMBLE

"London's Plantation in the Southern Part of Virginia," as the Jamestown settlement was officially called, must have seemed a paradise to the first settlers after months of being confined to the three tiny sailing ships. On April 26, 1607, as the colonists sighted the Virginia Capes, the expedition's chronicler, George Percy, recorded that:

> *The same day we entered into the bay of Chesupioc.... There we landed and discovered a little way, but wee could find nothing worth the speaking of, but faire meddowes and goodly tall Trees, with such Freshwaters running through the woods as I was almost ravished at the first sight thereof.*

The colonists devoted the next few days to exploring along the river, which they named after the king. Some 50 miles upstream they selected a place on the river's north bank—an island comprised largely of a tidal marsh bordered by a deep channel where they could bring the ships close to shore. The newcomers immediately set to work building a small fortified trading post, a store-

Sunset over the James River. Although often hostile and unforgiving, Virginia possessed a beauty that touched all. Its vast hardwood forests and abundant wildlife would seize the imagination of everyone who described it. Even today, the descriptions of scenes long vanished before the rush of civilization hold the reader's attention. The early writers indeed provided a chamber of commerce for this new world.

MAE SCANLAN

NPS—ARTIST: SIDNEY KING

The arrival of Lord De La Warr's large, well-supplied fleet saved Jamestown by the slimmest of margins! Having lost all but 60 of the 500 settlers during the previous winter, those remaining were ready to leave in the first relief ships when Lord De La Warr arrived with additional settlers and the desperately needed supplies.

house, a church, and some primitive wattle and daub thatched houses.

It did not take long for the settlers to discover that Tidewater Virginia was not the paradise it had first appeared to be. The brutal, muggy heat of summer, coupled with spoiled provisions, brackish drinking water, and disease-laden insects, created a situation in which only the fortunate survived. A malignant fever, believed to have been malaria, struck down many settlers. During the winter of 1607 - 08, more than half of the first band of settlers perished before the second group and sorely needed supplies arrived.

This devastating toll was a grim preview of what would occur over and over again during the first century of Virginia's colonization. The winter of 1609 - 10 unleashed the worst blow. Within a few months the struggling colony was reduced from 500 strong to 60 disheartened survivors. The arrival of a major relief party was all that saved Virginia from abandonment at this time.

The rescuers found the remaining colonists suffering from starvation and disease, their houses in ruins. The situation was so discouraging, in fact, that Sir Thomas Gates, captain of the fleet of ships bringing new colonists in 1610, ordered all

the survivors to board his ships for the return voyage to England.

As Gates was departing, he encountered a ship commanded by Lord Thomas De La Warr, a member of the king's council for Virginia. De La Warr countermanded Gates's decision, directed that all the colonists be put ashore, and, as governor, instituted strict disciplinary measures in an attempt to strengthen the colony's resolve to succeed. However, Sir Thomas Dale, who soon succeeded Lord De La Warr, wrote to the king that "Every man allmost laments himself of being here...."

The English attempt to settle in Virginia could succeed only if a number of problems were resolved. First, the Virginia Company of London, which had received a charter to establish and finance the settlement, was expected to earn a profit for its stockholders. The settlers experi-

The capitalists who funded the establishment of the Virginia colony may have been concerned with the glory of England and the spreading of the Anglican religion to the savages. But, above all they demanded that the new enterprise turn a profit. Tobacco eventually proved to be the economic base for Virginia for the next two centuries.

mented with a variety of products to find a source of urgently needed income for the colony.

Wine, silk, glass, pitch, tar, sassafras, and potash met with little or no success. Even after several years, the colony was still unable to turn a profit. Then John Rolfe improved the bitter native tobacco by crossing it with a West Indian variety that became popular with English smokers. It was this new tobacco that made it possible for the colony to grow and prosper.

The newcomers found that there was much more to survival in their new home than finding a successful cash crop. In the earlier years, they were frequently forced to find food or starve. While the Indians failed to hold this land, they left their mark upon it and upon the people who followed them. It was not until the settlers were able and willing to grow crops as did the Native Americans that hunger ceased to be a serious concern. The Indian's corn, combined with the English hog, provided the basic diet for Virginians for many generations.

Although most of Virginia was forested and provided an abundance of wood, construction of badly needed housing presented a serious problem. Not only did the colony lack skilled craftsmen to build quality housing, but the few who ventured into the newly settled area found that they often had to adapt to unfamiliar materials. It would be some time before most homes took on any air of permanence.

Within a decade the Virginia Company was under pressure to establish a legal system and a degree of colonial self-determination. Consequently, the company permitted establishment of a representative assembly with authority to enact local laws, subject to the company's veto power. This assembly, set up in Jamestown in 1619, was the first such representative law-making body in North America. Soon it passed laws for the observance of the Sabbath and the planting of food crops. Acting as a court, it also enforced its own laws by passing sentence upon violators of the law.

Struggling settlers also found themselves confronted by violence as a fact of life. Their constant friction with native inhabitants repeatedly hindered or set back their efforts to develop the

Virginia's survival and growth has been attributed to a number of factors. Few equal the contribution of Indian corn that provided an easily tended staple for the new settlers. Some species matured early in the season; others could be harvested late to provide food when the woods and streams provided little.

Few 17th-century figures capture the imagination as do Pocahontas and John Smith. Pocahontas was the Indian princess who helped save the colony as a child. Later kidnapped and converted to Christianity she married John Rolfe. On a visit to England she was introduced to the king and widely entertained. She died before she could return to Virginia. A professional soldier and explorer, John Smith's autocratic ways were needed to start the colony on the way to stability. His injury and return to England coupled with the disregard of his advice by the remaining colonists were directly responsible for the dreadful "starving time" during the winter of 1609 - 10.

colony. The slightest provocation on the part of either group could lead to a skirmish or open warfare. There were both English and Indians ready and willing to trample the property, rights, or lives of the other group.

The chief irritant causing these conflicts was the rapidly increasing expansion of settlement on and cultivation of lands claimed and used by the Indians. Expansion was encouraged by the Virginia Company, which sought to attract settlers to the colony. In some cases the new residents paid their own way. Others came, worked for the company, became tenant farmers, and were finally granted their lands outright.

BEYOND THE LIMITS OF JAMESTOWN

For the first 23 years the colonists generally restricted their activities to the James River. The early years of tobacco cultivation created a virtual gold rush not too different from the California Gold Rush of the mid-19th century. The colonists went wild planting tobacco, even cultivating plots in the streets of Jamestown.

This rush to plant was abruptly halted in 1622 when a major Indian uprising claimed the lives of 347 colonists, a third of the population, and wiped out most of the outlying settlements. The badly demoralized Virginians hung on grimly, reorganized, and during the next several years began an

CONNIE TOOPS

SHIRLEY M. WHITENACK

One of the industries the early Virginians tried was that of glassblowing. Both Polish (in 1608) and Italian (in 1620) glassblowers were brought to Virginia in attempts to make this a paying proposition. However, first the "starving time" of 1610 and later the Indian uprising of 1622 put an end to these efforts. Today these early crafts are demonstrated by skilled glassblowers and their products sold to support the operation.

offensive that nearly annihilated the Powhatan Confederation.

As a result of this devastating setback, the Virginia Company came under attack, and its royal charter was annulled in 1624. The glaring reality was that since 1607, of some 5,000 persons participating in the program to establish this colony, 4,000 had perished and another 300 had returned home. Virginia then became a crown colony under which the king appointed the colonial governor and council. As the king devoted almost no time to the distant colony, Virginia consequently experienced greater freedom.

With a growing population and money to be made in cultivating tobacco, the Virginians moved outward in a renewed rush to settle unoccupied lands. A major impetus behind the renewed period of land development was the so-called "head-right" system, which encouraged the creation of tobacco plantations in a pattern of widely dispersed settlement.

Under this system, a colonist desiring to become a planter could obtain 50 acres of virgin land, plus an additional 50 acres in return for each new colonist for whom he paid transportation costs from Britain to Virginia. Some successful planters were thus able to assemble sizeable plantations, expanding to hundreds, and eventually even thousands of acres.

The York River became the new frontier. As its fertile lands were quickly claimed, other settlers moved northward onto the next two peninsulas. This rapid movement of Virginia colonial expansion continued unabated until it encountered settlements of the new colony of Maryland along the Potomac River.

The expansion beyond the James River basin also changed Jamestown's role in colonial Virginia. Although originally no more than a military outpost of England, it quickly evolved as the major settlement in the region, with smaller communities nearby. As more settlements sprang up many miles away, Jamestown finally became the capital of what was a large and expanding colony.

Although it was no longer the military center or the single trading center, Jamestown now served as the legislative nucleus. By the mid-1600s the tiny capital boasted a red-brick state house, a brick church, and approximately 30 other buildings. The royal governor lodged in Jamestown or nearby, the few officials of the colony worked here, and the legislature gathered in its buildings.

When the assembly was not in session, the town was largely deserted. As new counties were formed, their own local governing bodies began to have an impact upon the citizen that the central government no longer had. When ships landed, the new arrivals normally paused only to orient themselves before rushing off to the frontier, where land and opportunities were available.

Jamestown was the capital of Virginia from 1607-1699. While the capital remained here for almost a century, the capitol buildings were not as long-lived. The fourth or last statehouse at Jamestown burned in 1698 giving those who were opposed to the capital's location the opportunity to push moving the seat of government to what would become Williamsburg.

JEFF GNASS

GROWING PAINS IN A NEW LAND

When Jamestown became the colonial capital, it also became the point of conflict between royal authority and the increasingly independent Virginians. The colonists, often forced to fend for and protect themselves, saw little reason why they should be controlled by anyone outside the colony.

Sir John Harvey, who came to Virginia as royal governor in 1630, learned this the hard way. His rather contentious and haughty nature, coupled with his disregard for the interests of his constituents, soon led to an impasse in which he was "thrust out" by the Virginians. He was sent back to England, where he succeeded in justifying his actions to the king. Not leaving well enough alone, he soon returned to Virginia to unleash his vengeance on the colonists. He was ultimately stripped of his office, and became so entangled in the courts that he was lucky to return to England with only the clothes on his back.

JEFF GNASS

Jamestown did not die—it only changed. In time the bulk of the island would belong to the Travis and Ambler families. These impressive ruins are all that remain of the Ambler's manor home. Damaged during two wars, it was finally burned in 1895.

of the old house of burgesses, and the convention adopted a constitution for an Independent Commonwealth of Virginia. In fact, many of the actions that led to America's eventual separation from England had their beginnings at Williamsburg.

Just as Williamsburg's influence was being felt far beyond the borders of Virginia, so the colony was expanding far beyond the flatlands of the Tidewater, into the foothills and into and over the mountains. But as Virginia grew, pressures increased for moving the capital nearer to the center of the vast area within its jurisdiction. Finally, in 1780 the capital was moved 60 miles farther inland to Richmond, on the James River, where it remains to this day.

The loss of the capital to the Tidewater was indicative of the economic decline that had gripped the lower Peninsula for half a century. By

the end of the Revolution, the soil of tobacco lands in eastern Virginia had become exhausted. Consequently, the planters had moved westward, taking with them the region's economic vitality.

There were always those who recognized Williamsburg's significant role in the nation's birth. But no steps were taken until after World War I, when W.A.R. Goodwin led the movement to bring the town back to life. Goodwin was the rector of Bruton Parish Church, and a member of the College of William and Mary faculty. He achieved only limited success with his dream until he was able to enlist the support of the famous philanthropist John D. Rockefeller, Jr.

After deciding that the project had merit, Rockefeller undertook to restore Williamsburg on a scale that must have astounded even Goodwin. He established an organization to secure and restore the town's historic area. It became the

The place of worship of the powerful families of Virginia for many generations, Bruton Parish Church would play its role in the Revolution. In the 20th century its pastor, W. A. R. Goodwin, envisioned Williamsburg restored and conveyed this to John D. Rockefeller, Jr. who made this dream a reality.

While Williamsburg was emerging as the new capital of the Colony, nearby Yorktown was becoming its most flourishing tobacco port. On the York River, it was a commercial center as well as the port of entry for the capital. The ferry to Gloucester Point also linked it with the rapidly expanding areas of northeastern Virginia. Not only tobacco but a wide range of agricultural and lumber products were shipped from here to pay for the necessities and luxuries that regularly arrived at the port.

largest project of this type anywhere, and has served as a prototype for historic restoration projects throughout the world.

To this day the Colonial Williamsburg Foundation continues to expand upon and refine the original concept and plans. Millions of visitors come to Williamsburg each year seeking to peer back to an earlier time. Not only the buildings and other physical features of Williamsburg are recreated, but also its lifestyle and crafts, through living history demonstrations portraying life in 18th-century Virginia.

YORKTOWN'S STAR RISES

Nicholas Martiau, a French Protestant, was one of the early settlers on the banks of the York River. He was granted the land upon which the town of York would be built almost 70 years later. Yorktown's excellent harbor and river crossing were recognized as great assets, and it was designated as one of a series of tobacco ports throughout coastal Virginia.

The new community's location adjacent to the rich tobacco lands of the York River basin, combined with easy access to the government at Williamsburg, attracted a number of capable and ambitious men. They arrived with the experience and capital necessary to move directly into large business ventures.

Fifty acres were surveyed into lots that were quickly sold to persons interested in investing or settling in the new community. Purchasers of lots were required to build upon them within a short time. Soon it was discovered that the original survey did not include the waterfront. The legislature later resolved this embarrassing situation by purchasing the waterfront land and designating it as a commons.

Yorktown became the county's social and administrative center. Soon the courthouse, the jail, the church, and the customhouse were located there. Yorktown's active port regularly cleared ships bound for Britain, Africa, the Canary Islands, the West Indies, and other ports along the North American coast.

It was inevitable that this leading commercial center would be politically active as well. Its major families, headed by the Nelsons, became influential at every level of government. Yorktown's leaders played a major role in the colony's government, most notably in the events leading to the Revolution.

Unlike other Virginia rivers, the York is very short. By the 1750s the tobacco lands along its

17

shore were exhausted of tobacco. With diminishing crops in the York River basin, Yorktown's trade and population had begun to decline. This might have been very gradual except that the Revolution, a score of years later, greatly accelerated the process.

FRICTION WITH THE MOTHER COUNTRY

Yorktown's political leaders helped lead the resistance to what they considered the British government's tyranny. The situation degenerated to such a degree that the royal governor, Lord Dunmore, seized the colony's ammunition supply in Williamsburg and placed it upon the British naval ship *Fowey*, anchored at Yorktown. This action so outraged the citizens that the governor decided to flee to the ship. The Fowey's commander threatened to bombard Yorktown if anyone attempted to prevent his escape. Governor Dunmore boarded the ship and sailed away, and with him went the last vestiges of royal government in Virginia.

War with Britain was imminent, and the newly formed state government repaired the badly deteriorated fortifications and stationed troops at Yorktown. The hostilities severely disrupted the town's way of life, prompting citizens to move their families and businesses inland. Poorly supplied and badly disciplined troops caused considerable damage to unoccupied properties. While peacetime commerce declined, commerce in support of the war kept the port and its citizenry very busy.

In 1780, British troops under Brigadier General Benedict Arnold began to raid up and down the James River. General George Washington countered by sending the Marquis de Lafayette to resist the British.

Events elsewhere were pointing toward a major confrontation in Virginia. General Sir Henry Clinton led British troops into the South, convinced that here lay an opportunity for success that had eluded him in the North. He believed that the Colonists would rally to the Crown if given the chance.

Within a few months Clinton had captured Charleston, thereby adding South Carolina to the area of Georgia already under British control. He then returned to New York, leaving Lord Charles Cornwallis in charge. Cornwallis moved aggressively to subdue the region. The Patriots, already disheartened by the loss at Charleston, were devastated by the defeat of troops at Camden, South Carolina, under General Horatio Gates, the American victor at Saratoga.

The Swan Tavern was the most prestigious place for the professionals of the community to meet, relax, and carry on business. Destroyed by the explosion of a Union ammunition dump in 1862, the National Park Service reconstructed it in 1934.

The corner of Nelson and Main is occupied by the Nelson House (foreground) and Session House (rear). These two homes represent the most significant and oldest remaining structures in Yorktown proper. The former was the home of a signer of the Declaration of Independence and the latter, constructed in 1699, is the oldest surviving house.

The Thomas Pate House was built in 1703 by a local ferryman. Later owned by the prominent Digges family, it was used as a rental property for many years. Restored in 1925, it is now owned by the National Park Service.

RUSS FINLEY

The Sommerwell House, built circa 1707, is typical of many of the houses of early Yorktown. It has been a residence, a tavern, a school, and in time a hospital, hotel, and park headquarters. The National Park Service policy is that if a structure is not used for exhibition purposes it should follow its original uses. Therefore, Sommerwell House is now a residence for a park employee, ensuring that the home's interior is as carefully preserved as possible.

With Washington's appointment of General Nathanael Greene to command in the South in late 1780, American fortunes immediately began to improve. Greene orchestrated a successful campaign that culminated in the bloody and bitterly fought Battle of Guilford Courthouse in North Carolina.

While Cornwallis was technically the victor, he found himself far from his base and with few supplies. Casualties had reduced his troops by

The home of Thomas "the Secretary" Nelson, the highest ranking civil servant in the colony. The finest home in Yorktown, it was selected by the British commander, Lord Cornwallis, as his headquarters. This quickly drew heavy Allied fire, and caused the elderly Secretary to flee his home for the safety of the Allied lines, never to occupy it again.

Looking northward along Yorktown's Main Street in 1781 before the battle started. The County Courthouse and Swan Tavern represent very prominent features. At the far end of the street is the Windmill, destined to be a landmark in upriver Yorktown for almost another century.

nearly one third, and the expected Loyalist support failed to materialize. He quickly moved to Wilmington, North Carolina, on the coast, where his forces were reinforced and resupplied.

Cornwallis then made a fateful decision. Convinced that the South could never be conquered while Virginia provided men and material, he decided to eliminate this source of supply. In the spring of 1781, Cornwallis moved northward into Virginia, joined British forces at Petersburg, and carried out raids throughout southern Virginia during the early summer.

WAR COMES TO YORKTOWN

Returning to the base at Portsmouth, Cornwallis received orders to seize and fortify a port in which big British naval vessels could spend the winter. Cornwallis decided that Yorktown would best serve the purpose, so he abandoned Portsmouth and moved north to the York River. He occupied the ports of York and Gloucester, and at a leisurely pace began to fortify them.

While Cornwallis had been in the South earlier, Washington had been outside the major British base in New York City. French General Comte de Rochambeau had arrived almost a year earlier with an excellent army to aid the American cause. Without naval support, however, the combined forces could not attack the strongly fortified British base.

With his army both underpaid and under-

The Battle of Chesapeake, fought on March 16, 1781, was the forerunner of the Battle of the Virginia Capes fought on September 5, 1781. It ensured Allied control of the Chesapeake Bay allowing the assembly of the Allied forces and cut Cornwallis off from escape by sea. It made the siege and victory at Yorktown possible.

manned, Washington was extremely frustrated by his inability to launch an attack. Fortunately, events were in motion that would change the situation. That winter Admiral Comte de Grasse sailed from France to the West Indies with a huge fleet. From the West Indies he sent word that he would arrive off the Virginia coast in the early fall. A period of feverish activity ensued as Washington and Rochambeau prepared to campaign in Virginia.

As the French admiral gathered his forces and sailed northward, fate was kind. The British fleet, which was supposed to shadow de Grasse's fleet, lost contact and unknowingly moved ahead of the French naval force. Arriving at Chesapeake Bay and finding no French ships, the British sailed on northward toward New York. This miscalculation allowed the French ships to reach the area, blockade the bay, and land troops to reinforce Lafayette, who was maintaining contact with Cornwallis.

Meanwhile, Washington and Rochambeau ingeniously tricked General Clinton into believing they were going to attack New York City. Consequently, while the 2,000 American and 5,000 French troops moved quickly southward through New Jersey, Pennsylvania, and Maryland, Clinton failed to send troops to aid Cornwallis at Yorktown.

Most of the Allied troops were at the head of Chesapeake Bay when word arrived that a British fleet had appeared off the coast, and that the French fleet under de Grasse had sailed out to engage it. All waited anxiously for word of the outcome.

British Admiral Sir Thomas Graves arrived off the Virginia capes on September 5, 1781, and the French fleet sailed out of the Chesapeake to attack the British. In the short engagement that followed, not a single ship was lost by either side, although both sustained casualties and some serious damage.

For the next several days the combatants drifted southward, watching each other. De Grasse

The siege of Yorktown was fought with the shovel and the cannon. The guns of this battery and others carried out the Allied bombardment which weakened the British forces and their will to fight.

RUSS FINLEY

then turned his ships northward and reestablished the blockade of the Chesapeake, while the British naval forces returned to New York for repairs and reinforcements. During the battle and its aftermath, a French fleet from Newport, Rhode Island, slipped into the bay with the big siege cannon that made possible the attack on Yorktown.

Returning to Chesapeake Bay, de Grasse sent ships to move soldiers and supplies from Maryland to the James River. The Allied troops were soon assembled at Williamsburg, ready to attack Cornwallis at Yorktown.

Washington advanced the 17,500 Allied troops against Cornwallis's troops, encircled the posts of York and Gloucester, and began a siege of York. As soon as preparations could be made, 8,300 Allied soldiers began to dig the first lines and batteries. By October 9, the big guns began to roar. This bombardment continued without letup for nine days.

Once the British defenses of Yorktown were sufficiently weakened, the Allies began a second, and much closer, siege line. This trench line was delayed because the British forces still held two enclosed fortification sites, called redoubts, below town. On the night of October 14, American and French troops stormed the earthworks and completed the second siege line. This effectively sealed Cornwallis's fate. Attempts to delay the Allied siege operations and bring about escape were now futile.

When Cornwallis concluded that he could expect no relief from Clinton in New York, he requested the terms of surrender on October 17. The following day, commissioners met at the home of Augustine Moore within the Allied lines to negotiate the articles of capitulation. The document was signed on October 19, 1781, and the British Army laid down its arms that afternoon.

Even the least perceptive participant could hardly have failed to grasp the full impact of the victory at Yorktown. When news reached Great Britain that one third of its army in America had surrendered at Yorktown, public opinion solidified against the war.

Those who had opposed the war from its very beginning gained the upper hand, and in a short time a political party came to power determined to have peace. This led to negotiations and ultimately to the Treaty of Paris, which gave the Americans peace and independence. Thus the British Colonial period virtually ended at Yorktown, a scant 20 miles from Jamestown where it had begun.

SUGGESTED READING

DAVIS, BURKE. *The Campaign that Won America: The Story of Yorktown.* New York: Eastern Acorn Press, 1982.

EVANS, EMORY G. *Thomas Nelson of Yorktown, Revolutionary Virginian.* Williamsburg: The Colonial Williamsburg Foundation (distributed by the University Press of Virginia, Charlottesville, Virginia), 1975.

JOHNSTON, HENRY P. *The Yorktown Campaign and the Surrender of Cornwallis, 1781.* New York: Eastern Acorn Press, 1975.

MORGAN, EDMUND S. *American Slavery, American Freedom. The Ordeal of Colonial Virginia.* New York: W.W. Norton & Company Inc., 1975.

A legend in his own time! George Washington was the supreme Allied commander at Yorktown. He was able to weld the French and American armies into an effective force to surround and reduce Lord Cornwallis's British and German forces at Yorktown.

Dreams Pursued and Realized

RUSS FINLEY

Americans, faced with the task of building a nation, soon lost sight of the significance of what had occurred at Yorktown. There would be little recognition until many years later. Eventually the efforts of a few farsighted individuals focused national attention upon the Historic Triangle.

Yorktown received some early but fleeting recognition. On October 29, 1781, five days after receiving news of the Allied victory at Yorktown, the Continental Congress resolved: "That the United States in Congress assembled, will cause to be erected at York, in Virginia, a marble column...." Over a century would elapse before this monument would become a reality.

This unimposing room saw the preparation of the terms of surrender of the British Army. The events here set in motion the forces leading to America's freedom.

It was here on October 18, 1781, in the home of Augustine Moore, that the terms of surrender were prepared. This house survived two sieges and served as the center for the first major celebration of the surrender in 1881.

Preceding pages: The Grand French Battery rained shot and shell on Yorktown day and night. Photo by Russ Finley.

In the 1880s, the upcoming 100th anniversary of British surrender at Yorktown generated a new wave of interest. The Yorktown Centennial Association was established to plan and organize a major celebration.

The cornerstone of the long-awaited Victory Monument was laid during the anniversary observance in 1881, and the column was completed three years later. The association then acquired an option on the Temple Farm tract containing the historic Moore House, intending to donate it to the nation as a park. The centennial celebration proved to be a historic event, with President Chester A. Arthur and other national and European dignitaries in attendance. But the attempt to establish a federally administered military park did not succeed.

JAMESTOWN IS RECOGNIZED

To honor the Jamestown experience there were similar sporadic and mildly successful efforts, generally paralleling those at Yorktown. Local events, sponsored by the nearby College of William and Mary, included the 200th anniversary celebrated in 1807, the "Virginiad" in 1822, and in 1857 the 250th anniversary, which attracted nearly 10,000 spectators. The highlight of the latter ceremony was a speech by former president John Tyler in which he stated:

> ...as the first impress of the Anglo-Saxon was made on this beach, so the first impulse to independence was given at Williamsburg and the last battle for Liberty was fought at Yorktown.

The Civil War abruptly halted further efforts to recognize the site of Jamestown. In 1889, the Association of the Preservation of Virginia Antiquities was established. It soon acquired nearly 23 acres surrounding the historic church on Jamestown Island. Several years later, federal funds were appropriated for the erection of a seawall to halt erosion, which posed a serious threat to the church's site.

With the 300th anniversary only two years away, in 1905 Congress appropriated $50,000 "for a permanent monument upon the place of the first

Authorized in 1781, begun in 1881 and completed in 1884, the monument to Victory and Alliance stands today as a fitting symbol of the combined French and American effort that made the victory at Yorktown possible.

JEFF GNASS

permanent English settlement at Jamestown, Virginia." The Tercentenary Monument was completed on schedule for the anniversary year.

A major exposition was held, marking the first time that Jamestown had been the focus of national attention. Unfortunately, most of the activities occurred not on Jamestown Island, but 50 miles away in present-day Norfolk. Jamestown itself gained only the monument, and a building designated as a rest house for travelers daring to visit the isolated site.

ESTABLISHING A PARK

During the early 20th century, bills were regularly introduced into Congress to establish Jamestown as a park, but the coming of World War I once again turned the nation's attention elsewhere. Local interests sought in vain to obtain national recognition for the Triple Shrines as a complete historic unit. However, there were forces already in motion at this time that would ultimately lead to the establishment of the Colonial National Historical Park.

One of these forces was the growth of the national park movement. Strong conservation sentiment in this country after the Civil War had led to establishment of a number of national parks, beginning with Yellowstone in 1872. A growing concern for the country's pre-Columbian and natural-phenomena sites had also led to passage of the Antiquities Act in 1906. Under this act a number of national monuments were established by presidential proclamation beginning with Devils Tower National Monument in Wyoming. Even though there was a substantial array of parks and monuments by the second decade of the 20th century, no single agency existed to manage them. It was not until 1916 that the situation was remedied by congressional establishment of the National Park Service.

When Horace M. Albright was named as the second park service director in 1929, he identified his intention to "go heavily into the historical park field." He felt that the nation's natural and historical jewels belonged within the same system.

Albright's early efforts to bring historical areas into the park system ran into determined resistance from factions within the War Department, which administered the Civil War battlefield parks. Later, however, with strong public and congressional support, he took advantage of two opportunities that suddenly arose.

First, an association had been formed to honor George Washington on the 200th anniversary of

It was not until 1907 that Jamestown started to receive national and international attention. This monument was a product of the Jamestown Exposition of 1907. Because Jamestown lacked the facilities necessary for a major event, the actual exposition was held in present-day Norfolk, Virginia. The monument commemorating the 300th anniversary still stands on the island today.

ED COOPER

his birth by reconstructing his birthplace at Wakefield on the Potomac River. This organization was seeking federal assistance to carry out the project. Albright's friends steered the group toward the National Park Service.

Second, the 150th anniversary of the victory at Yorktown would occur in 1931. Plans were underway to make this a major national and international event. Astute individuals felt that this was the time to press for a single major park incorporating two of the three elements of the Triple Shrines. Williamsburg's ongoing restoration by a private foundation would complete the triad. A scenic roadway would be built to connect all three sites. Albright eagerly embraced both projects and set out to bring these areas into the national park system.

It is questionable whether this federal undertaking would have been possible without the Rockefeller interest in Williamsburg. The decision several years earlier of John D. Rockefeller, Jr. to take on the landmark restoration of Colonial Williamsburg was already focusing national attention on the Peninsula area.

On July 3, 1930, Congress passed an act authorizing the president to establish Colonial National Monument by proclamation. President Herbert Hoover did so on December 30, 1930.

Dr. H. J. Eckenrode, historian for the Virginia Commission on Conservation and Development, and an active participant in the establishment of the park, succinctly described the culmination of efforts to preserve the Triple Shrines for the nation:

> *The establishment of the Colonial National Monument was the result of a great idea carried through energetically and quickly. Delay would have frustrated it; a happy combination of circumstances and determination brought it to success. Beyond doubt it will be the greatest historical park in the world, a beautiful and impressive memorial to the most important events in American history.*

From a Dream to a Reality

Early in 1931 Oliver G. Taylor, appointed engineer-in-charge, *activated* Colonial National Monument. A yet-to-be designated superintendent was to take over management of the park after the sesquicentennial celebration in October. The challenges facing the new unit's staff were staggering. Three major matters required immediate attention: land purchases necessary to form the nucleus of the park; planning, surveying, and constructing facilities needed for the upcoming celebration; and selection of a route and the start of construction of the roadway that would tie together the Historic Triangle.

Director Albright also had some difficult questions to resolve. Now that the Park Service had acquired a historical area, it faced the challenge of managing it under the mandates of the National Park Service's enabling legislation. The Park Service had to prove to skeptics that an organization previously focused exclusively on the western states could effectively manage an extensive historical preservation program in the East.

First it was essential to develop policies for the management of historical areas. A staff then had to be recruited and trained at both national and park levels to carry out those policies. It was quickly apparent, however, that the distance between Yellowstone and Yorktown was vast both ideologically and geographically.

By early summer William Robinson, Jr. was appointed the first superintendent of Colonial. He was a civil engineer by profession, and an expert on Confederate privateers. Two assistant park historians were also recruited to carry out urgently needed research.

Together with the rapid approach of the sesquicentennial, the sheer excitement of a new concept, a new park, and a new staff was exhilarating. The employees found themselves quickly thrust into the midst of this challenging enterprise. Because of competing demands of administrative and public relations functions that required immediate attention, the historians found that time for research was scarce.

During this period land acquisition moved along rapidly, and soon most of the needed lands were in federal possession. Under Taylor's able direction federal, state, and local governments worked cooperatively to ensure that the area could efficiently host the thousands of visitors who would attend the celebration. It was a race against time, but it all came together.

Although Yorktown was the focal point of most celebration activities, the Colonial Parkway right-of-way had to be selected, acquired, and surveyed before construction could begin. Director Albright succeeded in persuading President Hoover to transfer U.S. Navy lands along the York River to the National Park Service for the first section of Colonial Parkway.

By the summer of 1931 the route had been designated and contracts had been let for clearing, landfilling, and bridge construction through the Yorktown Naval Mine Depot. But it was not until

Begun in 1921, the Colonial Parkway would ultimately stretch from Jamestown Island to the bluffs below Yorktown. This is a view from the earliest section to be constructed along the York River in the vicinity of the Naval Weapons Station.

1957 that parkway construction was completed.

The sesquicentennial celebration went off as scheduled in October of 1931. Between October 16 and 19, approximately 250,000 visitors came to Yorktown to take part in the many activities. Such a major event in an area that only a few months earlier would have been ill prepared was a tribute to the energy and commitment of all involved.

HELP FROM THE CCC

By October 20, 1931, Taylor turned over control of the park to Superintendent Robinson. While Colonial's employees might have anticipated a period of quiet in which to learn their craft in an orderly fashion, this was not to happen. This was the height of the Great Depression, and President Franklin D. Roosevelt was determined to put the nation back to work. Thus began the era of "Alphabet Soup Agencies" and much needed help for natural and historical conservation projects.

Consequently, Colonial National Monument was in the forefront of the reemployment effort. There were times when as many as five Civilian Conservation Corps (CCC) camps comprising up

The numerous tidal creeks, streams, and marshes made the design and construction of the Colonial Parkway very difficult. However, the same features today make traveling the parkway a memorable experience regardless of the season or time of day. We now appreciate the marshes' contribution not only to beauty but to our quality of life.

to 1,000 men were based at Colonial. With men, funds, and orders to proceed, the new managers jumped to their appointed tasks. During the next eight years the vision of Colonial National Historical Park progressed far toward becoming a reality.

The parkway was completed from the Fusilier's Redoubt at Yorktown to the tunnel beneath Williamsburg's historic district. At Yorktown the historic Moore and Sommerwell houses were restored, while Swan Tavern, the Medical Shop, and their outbuildings were reconstructed. The earthworks of the Allied siege lines were researched and reconstructed, then a tour road was built through these siege lines and the camps. A system of historical signs was researched, designed, and installed throughout the park.

Virtually all of Jamestown Island was acquired in 1934 by the National Park Service, and the Jamestown Archaeological Project was established to explore the area's buried features. In 1936, Congress redesignated the approximately 9,000-acre national monument as Colonial National Historical Park.

One of the major projects undertaken at Yorktown in the 1950s was that of researching, locating, and reconstructing British Redoubt #10. Captured by the Americans on the night of October 14, 1781, and incorporated into the Second Allied Siege Line, this work was leveled by Washington's orders. The fall of Redoubt #10 and neighboring Redoubt #9 convinced Cornwallis that his position at Yorktown was perilous and ultimately led to his surrender.

ROBERT K. ANDER

Just how much more could have been accomplished with a continuing investment of such vast resources of men and money will never be known, for an improving domestic economy brought on by World War II in Europe began to sharply curtail conservation projects in the late 1930s. The attack on Pearl Harbor in 1941 effectively ended this era of great progress at Colonial. One employee after another departed for military service or defense work until only a skeleton staff operated the park. The parkway was closed to civilian traffic, and park activities were reduced to a minimum.

FRENCH CEMETERY

This simple cross is thought to mark the burial place of about 50 unidentified French soldiers killed during the Siege of Yorktown.

LINDA GALLO FETZER

ANNIVERSARIES SPARK A REVIVAL

During the mid-1950s, local, state, and federal agencies and groups were starting to plan for a major commemoration of the 350th anniversary of Jamestown's founding. This planning rejuvenated park research-and-development programs emphasizing Jamestown. Construction of the parkway was completed from Williamsburg to Jamestown Island at the south end, and to the York River bluffs at the north end.

Major visitor centers were designed and completed at both Jamestown and Yorktown, and structures were restored in Yorktown. A number of archaeological investigations were undertaken to clarify some key interpretive stories. The sheer magnitude of the work accomplished in a relatively short time is once again a tribute to all of those who participated.

Yorktown became a focal point as the 200th anniversary of the American victory drew near. Planning proceeded somewhat leisurely until a presidential decision concentrated all the nation's bicentennial celebrations in 1976. A period of frantic activity followed at Colonial as the park sought to complete in 1975 all the programs previously scheduled for 1981.

Located along the heavily-wooded yellow tour road at Yorktown, this simple cross provides a fitting memorial to 50 French soldiers who gave their lives here. A gift from French veterans, it replicates the crosses over the graves of American dead in cemeteries in France.

Development and construction there included expansion of both visitor centers, upgrading the parkway, and restoration of the Nelson, Smith, and Ballard houses and other structures. In spite of all these preparations, the number of visitors at Yorktown, as elsewhere in the nation, fell far short of projections.

By the late 1970s there was substantial public interest in holding a 1981 celebration at Yorktown patterned after the 1931 sesquicentennial. For four eventful days in 1981, several hundred thousand visitors came to witness numerous commemorative pageants, exhibits, and dedications. The excitement built to the climactic final day, when President Ronald Reagan marked the end of the observance with these words:

The commemoration of this battle marks the end of the revolution and the beginning of a new world era. The promise made on July 4th was kept on October 19th.

The dream described in that Pennsylvania hall was fulfilled on this Virginia field. Through courage, the support of our allies, and by the gracious hand of God, a revolution was won, a people set free and the world witnessed the most exciting adventure in the history of nations: the beginning of the United States of America.

SUGGESTED READING

Billings, Warren M., Ed. *The Old Dominion in the Seventeenth Century, A Documentary History of Virginia.* Williamsburg Virginia: Institute of Early American History and Culture (Published by the University of North Carolina Press, Chapel Hill), 1981.

Billings, Warren M. *Jamestown and the Founding of the Nation.* Gettysburg, Pennsylvania: Thomas Publications, 1991.

DAVID MUENCH

The southern boundary of the field in which the surrender occurred is the road running from Yorktown south to Warwick Courthouse. Today one can see that road and view "Surrender Field" from the overlook in the distance.

ED COOPER

The very symbol of royal authorization, the original building of the Governor's Palace was begun in 1710 and not completed until 1720. It was derisively called the "Palace" because of the taxes raised to build it. The building was destroyed by fire in 1781. Reconstruction upon its original foundations was begun in 1930 by the Colonial Williamsburg Foundation.

Williamsburg

Known worldwide, the restoration of the Colonial capital began in 1926, and has continued to this day with plans for the future. W. A. R. Goodwin, the pastor of Bruton Parish Church, conveyed his dream of a restored Williamsburg to John D. Rockefeller, Jr., so inspiring him that he undertook the restoration on a scale that must have amazed even Goodwin. The early efforts have grown into a huge complex that preserves and interprets the story of Virginia's second capital. Each year hundreds of thousands of visitors from all over the world come to Williamsburg to experience a sense of life in 18th-century Virginia. This experience is gained by touring the restored buildings—complete with historic furnishings—or attending a wide range of educational activities revolving around both everyday life and special happenings in the Colonial capital.

Created as a military outpost in the 1630s, regular or militia soldiers were always a part of the Williamsburg scene. These numbers swelled during periods of peace. However, as the center of a colony that stretched to the banks of the Ohio, there were continual problems between the aggressive frontiersmen and the Indians fighting to hold their land and way of life.

DAVID MUENCH

Williamsburg's period as the capital of the colony saw tremendous changes from the period that British troops were welcomed as defenders against the French until a later time when they were the enemy.

CONNIE TOOPS

Williamsburg seeks to introduce its visitors to life in the 18th century through both the reenactment of day-to-day life as well as special occasions. One of these is that of public times.

Government generated paper work in the 18th century much as it does today. The combination of government, commerce, and learning found at Williamsburg ensured that a printer would be needed here.

During the 18th century many services had to be available locally. One in particular was the grinding of grain into flour or meal. Early Virginia had both wind- and water-powered mills.

Service in the militia was required of all male colonists from adolescents to the elderly. At public times the militia was assembled and drilled. The drill seen today is probably more proficient and the participants better armed than in those times.

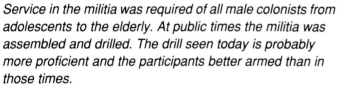

The weapons and munitions belonging to the colony were stored and repaired in the central magazine. The militia would assemble here during times of crisis.

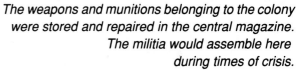

MAE SCANLAN

The apothecary shop was the center for the medical attempts to cure the many diseases that assailed the colonists.

In a time when there was no radio, television, or frequent newspapers, the only efficient means of quickly disseminating official information was by the town crier.

37

Beauty Amidst Tradition

While visitors may come to Colonial National Historical Park primarily to see its historical features and learn about nationally significant events of the past, their visit will be enhanced by an added dimension—the beautiful scenery and natural values of the present. It seems ironic that the natural environment, which proved to be such a harsh adversary to the early settlers, should today provide such a pleasing background for their historical legacy.

Across this gently rolling landscape, embraced by the tidal waters of the James and York rivers, the ebb and flow of the seasons spreads an ever-changing tapestry of color and form.

Scattered throughout the area are a wealth of gardens and flower beds. These can bloom from early spring to late fall.

FLORA AND FAUNA

Spring bursts forth with bright blossoms of a multitude of flowers and delicate hues of unfolding leaves. The white-bracted blossoms of the flowering dogwood tree transform expanses of woodland to a springtime "snowstorm," interrupted here and there with patches of pinkish-purple flowers of the eastern redbud tree. The forest floor is alive with the colors of the yellow-flowered adder's-tongue or the trout-lily, and of the pink lady's-slipper, a variety of orchid.

Summer offers the damp richness of lush vegetation—from the tidal marshlands to the darkly shaded forests. Autumn brings an end to the predominance of greens by painting the land with shades of yellow, brown, scarlet, and purple. Even winter's apparent bleakness of gray and brown against a dark evergreen counterpoint of pines and cedars lends a certain subtle and elemental charm to the countryside.

There is another type of ebb and flow that coincides with the change of seasons: the many species of wildlife that inhabit or visit the park. In spring, birds of many colors and sizes flood into the woodlands from tropical and subtropical wintering habitats far to the south.

As in the colonial period, the warblers, thrushes, flycatchers, and vireos, the scarlet tanager, indigo bunting, and northern oriole fill the land with a concert of musical songs. John Smith wrote of the redwing blackbirds, which continue to sing their melodious springtime songs from the marshes. In autumn, other migrants come south to

The Colonial Parkway is more than a corridor to link history. It is a passage through hardwood forests, tidal creeks, marshlands, and river overlooks. The spring masses of white dogwoods and redbud, the wealth of fall's colors framed in evergreens, and even the stark lines and shades of winter make the trip an unforgettable one.

The park is enriched by the presence of many species of bird life. The Carolina chickadee is one of these.

KENT & DONNA DANNEN

The park is on the Atlantic flyway and at times its shores are filled with waterfowl such as these mallards resting and feeding during their travels.

KENT & DONNA DANNEN

WILLIAM S. LEA

Interesting to watch, the groundhogs have proliferated within the park. Whether amidst the foundations of early Jamestown or on the earthworks around Yorktown, they find the good life here in increasing numbers.

the Chesapeake Bay area—flocks of geese and ducks drift in by the tens of thousands. Visitors may experience a special thrill in glimpsing a flock of the large white whistling swans gliding over the marshes, a bald eagle soaring majestically overhead, an osprey swooping down to snatch a fish from the river surface, or a great blue heron flapping lazily on its way from one marshy hunting ground to another.

There are two species that the early colonists surely not only saw, but quite likely also depended upon to help supply some of their food. They are the wild turkey, which can be seen in small flocks in the park today, and the bobwhite quail, whose distinctive "whistled" call carries far across the countryside.

Although generally harder to discern than avian species, many varieties of mammals inhabit Colonial. Visitors who look carefully may spot an opossum plucking persimmons in the autumn, young raccoons at play, kits of either the gray or red fox trailing behind their mother, or a pair of whitetail deer fawns silently observing their new world. Groundhogs abound in the park. In fact, from a historic preservation viewpoint, these large rodents create a problem by digging numerous burrows throughout the military earthwork fortifications.

There is a third kind of ebb and flow at Colonial, occurring over longer spans of time than the other two. The landscape evolved from a preponderance of forests when the first colonists arrived to the predominance of cultivated lands in the rush to grow tobacco. In recent decades the land has been returning to woodlands as abandoned fields are reclaimed by trees.

Much of the land surrounding the park is again in the process of massive change—toward extensive urban development. But within the park itself the trend is back to natural reforestation. Areas that were mostly open land during historic periods, such as the battlefields in the attack upon British-held Yorktown, have been taken over by forest. Now the National Park Service is studying how best to restore and maintain some of these historic landscapes.

Jamestown Island, the starting point of Colonial's story, is a splendid example of this often subtle blending of historic and natural landscapes. Clinging to the James River's north shore by the thin thread of a man-made isthmus, this low-lying island is the product of a series of ancient sandbars that have become ridges linked by marshes. "Ridge" is perhaps too generous a term, for these often isolated slivers of land, adorned with pines and an occasional oak or maple, are never more than a few dozen feet above sea level.

The extensive bodies of water in and around the park provide an excellent environment for animals such as the raccoon. They are found throughout the park taking advantage of the wide variety of foods available to them.

Jamestown Island has numerous vistas of its water along the tour roads. Here one can almost imagine what this must have been like when John Smith or other early settlers passed this way exploring and producing a livelihood while laying the foundations for a nation.

All that remained above ground of the Jamestown of the 17th century was the tower of the church of 1639. To honor those early pioneers the National Society of the Colonial Dames of America Daughters of the American Revolution built the existing Memorial Church over the original foundations.

Jamestown's charm results largely from this marriage of land and water.

The upper, westerly portion of the island, including the Jamestown site itself, clearly bears the imprint of man. The site of the first settlement stretches three quarters of a mile along the south shore. The voracious waters of the river, which in the past have eroded part of the townsite and the location of the original Fort James, have been held at bay during this century by a seawall and riprapping along part of the shore.

Pitch and Tar Swamp, ending in a marshy area called the Vale, borders the townsite on the north and west, while Orchard Run, a small marshy drainage from the swamp, borders the site on the east.

A CONGLOMERATION OF HISTORY

Jamestown is more a conglomeration of history than an example of any single period. Here are the vestiges of every century of European occupation and American history. The 17th century is typified most conspicuously by the church tower, the only remaining above-ground structure from the earliest years. Beyond lie a number of building foundations and the graveyard.

The 18th century is represented by the imposing ruins of the Ambler mansion. The 19th century's most impressive remains are the ruins of a Confederate fort, one of a number of Civil War defensive works built to deny the invading Union Army passage up the James River.

With the obvious exception of the National Park Service's Jamestown visitor center, the most impressive structures are the various forms of early 20th-century monumentation: the 300th anniversary monument (a small version of the Washington Monument obelisk in the nation's capital); and statues of Capt. John Smith and Pocahontas, daughter of Indian Chief Powhatan and wife of John Rolfe, an English planter.

Scattered around these reminders of earlier times is an attractive mixture of giant poplars, oaks, and smaller decorative trees such as dogwood and crape myrtle, an Asian tree. Trails, ditches, and roadways provide access throughout the area, and define the locations of early property lines.

The downstream, easterly portion of Jamestown Island presents a far wilder scene. While it is evident that man has been there, his imprint is steadily fading. The three- and five-

WILLIAM S. LEA

The early settlers reported a wilderness teeming with wildlife. The red fox today finds it a refuge in the midst of a rapidly growing urban area.

MAE SCANLAN

mile loop drives pass through an area formerly devoted to agriculture. It is now evolving through the cycle of regrowth toward climax forest. Beyond the edge of the road corridor are wild expanses of tidal marshland, such as Passmore Marsh, which are virtually impassable either on foot or by boat.

This near-wilderness part of the island provides a degree of privacy for wildlife not available in more heavily visited areas of the park. Musk-rats, otters, red foxes, and a profusion of birdlife live there. A short trail leads from the road to the outermost end of the island at Black Point, from which visitors may enjoy a sweeping panorama of the river.

It is within this especially wild and tranquil part of the park that visitors may best gain an awareness of the feelings a 17th-century English colonist, used to the more disciplined and tamed landscapes of his homeland, must have experi-

There is no better way to experience Jamestown Island than to travel its tour roads. Here its terrain and wildlife unfold before you. Rustic bridges take you across placid swamps or tidal creeks. You journey through hardwood glades or stands of pine recalling the land as first seen by the settlers.

RUSS FINLEY

enced. We may find such places a welcome respite from the fast pace of 20th-century urban life. Those first settlers must have looked upon the Virginia Tidewater wilderness with less of a sense of appreciation for its beauty and more of a fear of the vast unknown, and a desire to subdue and control their awesome new environment.

The Jamestown settlers needed products to both use and export. The many craft experiments here are still recalled through demonstrations of potting and glassmaking.

43

Nothing typifies the passage of time better than the giant oaks that have presided over the changes of such a large number of years. These "great oaks" just outside of Williamsburg represent a type of permanence in the midst of a constant chain of events.

JOURNEY ON THE COLONIAL PARKWAY

At the southern end of the Colonial Parkway the journey begins after the visitor passes over the isthmus connecting the island with the mainland. For more than 20 miles the scenic drive is filled with contrasts. First, it follows the bank of the James River, crossing tidal creeks such as Powhatan and Mill, and expanses of salt marsh; then it threads through wild forested acres.

Throughout this drive there is a constantly changing array of trees—in some stretches dense old-growth forest dominates while elsewhere there are more open areas of younger trees and shrubs, where only a few years ago there were open fields or cultivated lands. Here and there clusters of white-barked American sycamore or white poplar provide a clue that a home once stood upon a particular spot. These reminders are a bright contrast to the pines that frame them.

The parkway passes beneath Williamsburg's historic district via a tunnel, then traverses more woodlands on a series of curves that end at Felgate's Creek. From here nearly all the rest of the way into Yorktown the traveler can view the sweeping panorama of the York River off to the left. The York provides an exciting contrast to the woodlands along its banks.

In a matter of minutes this broad and changeable expanse of tidal water can change dramatically from a sparkling silvery-blue sheen to a threatening somber gray. Placid one moment, it can suddenly be dotted with whitecaps the next. Such is the case when a tremendous summer thunderstorm sweeps down upon Tidewater, unleashing wild gusts of wind and sheets of rain amid blinding flashes of lightning. The thunderclaps are reminiscent of the booming of cannon during the historic battles here.

Across Yorktown Creek the vista widens toward the northern end of the parkway. Directly ahead lie the earthworks, a reminder of the days when first the Americans and the French, and later the Union Army, besieged the town. On the left the first buildings of the village of Yorktown come into view.

THE COMMUNITY OF YORKTOWN

The attractiveness and charm of this community differs from that of other parts of the park. In contrast to the natural environment on Jamestown Island and along the parkway, Yorktown combines the dignified aging of its colonial buildings with the maturing of trees and other decorative plant life. Even though much of the flora around town is not native to Virginia, it is harmonious with the structures and the sense of history they engender. This blending has produced a beautiful and tasteful unity enriched by the passage of time.

Along the banks of Tobacco Road valley, which forms the eastern boundary of the village, a grove of bamboo grows side by side with native trees of this area. Yorktown's architecture of red-brick and white-frame Georgian-style houses is enhanced by a wide variety of trees and shrubs.

Along the streets, for instance, not only the native red mulberry trees flourish, but also the white mulberry—originally brought to America from China in the early 17th century for feeding silkworms in an attempt to establish a silk industry in the Colonies. Elsewhere are paper mulberry trees, a species introduced from Asia by way of Britain in the mid-18th century.

The crape myrtle has also adapted well, adding its beauty to Yorktown with pinkish late-summer flowers and pale orange autumn foliage that highlight the tree's silvery trunk.

THE BATTLEFIELD TOUR ROADS

Leaving Yorktown, the battlefield tour roads wind through military earthworks now softened by time; bordered by a cavalcade of wooded stretches interspersed now and then with open

MAE SCANLAN

The tour roads at Yorktown wander through history. The reconstructed Allied siege lines, encampments, and staging areas are intermixed with Civil War entrenchments in woods and marshlands. One of the most critical features is that of the Grand American Battery of the Second Siege Line. The construction of this battery caused Cornwallis to first attempt escape and then negotiate his Army's surrender.

pastures or cultivated fields, and occasionally by a creek or swamp. The woodland landscapes themselves vary from ancient stands of trees to areas only recently covered with red cedar and scrub-pine thickets.

The tour route passes Wormley Pond, an attractive expanse of freshwater behind a dam with a tidal creek directly below it. The pond magically mirrors the changing seasons of encircling trees and other vegetation. When the sun shines warmly on the pond's cool waters, resident turtles occupy every log to "catch the rays."

The tour roads first curve through the areas of the first and second siege lines, and then into locations where the Allied armies camped during the Revolutionary War. Throughout this part of the park, the impression of man's presence is stronger in the fields or in areas that once were fields.

Many visitors prefer to see the park by other means than the automobile. Here cyclists inspect Wormley Pond. The dam provided a crossing for American troops moving between their camps and the siege lines.

45

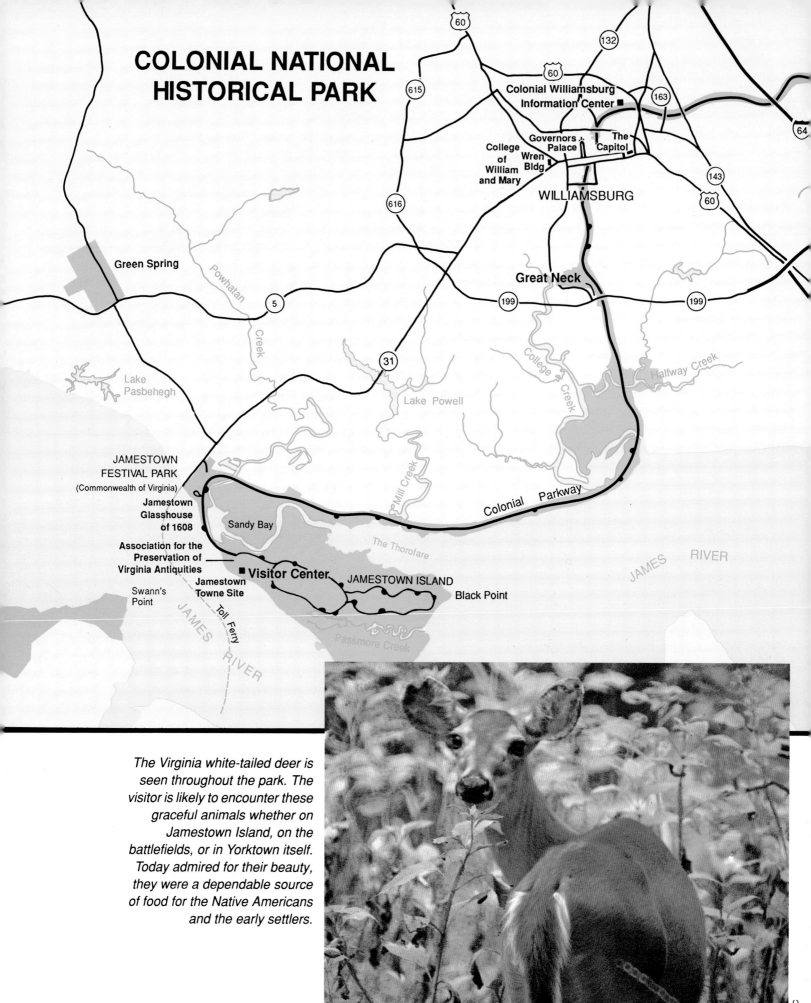

COLONIAL NATIONAL HISTORICAL PARK

60

132

615

60

Colonial Williamsburg
Information Center

163

College
of
William
and Mary

Governors
Palace

Wren
Bldg.

The
Capitol

64

WILLIAMSBURG

143

616

60

Green Spring

Powhatan

Creek

5

Great Neck

199

199

Lake
Pasbehegh

31

Lake Powell

College

Creek

Halfway Creek

JAMESTOWN
FESTIVAL PARK
(Commonwealth of Virginia)

Jamestown
Glasshouse
of 1608

Sandy Bay

Mill Creek

Colonial   Parkway

The Thorofare

JAMES   RIVER

Association for the
Preservation of
Virginia Antiquities

Swann's
Point

■ Visitor Center

Jamestown
Towne Site

JAMESTOWN ISLAND

Black Point

JAMES

RIVER

Toll
Ferry

Passmore Creek

The Virginia white-tailed deer is seen throughout the park. The visitor is likely to encounter these graceful animals whether on Jamestown Island, on the battlefields, or in Yorktown itself. Today admired for their beauty, they were a dependable source of food for the Native Americans and the early settlers.

JOHN OREHOVEC

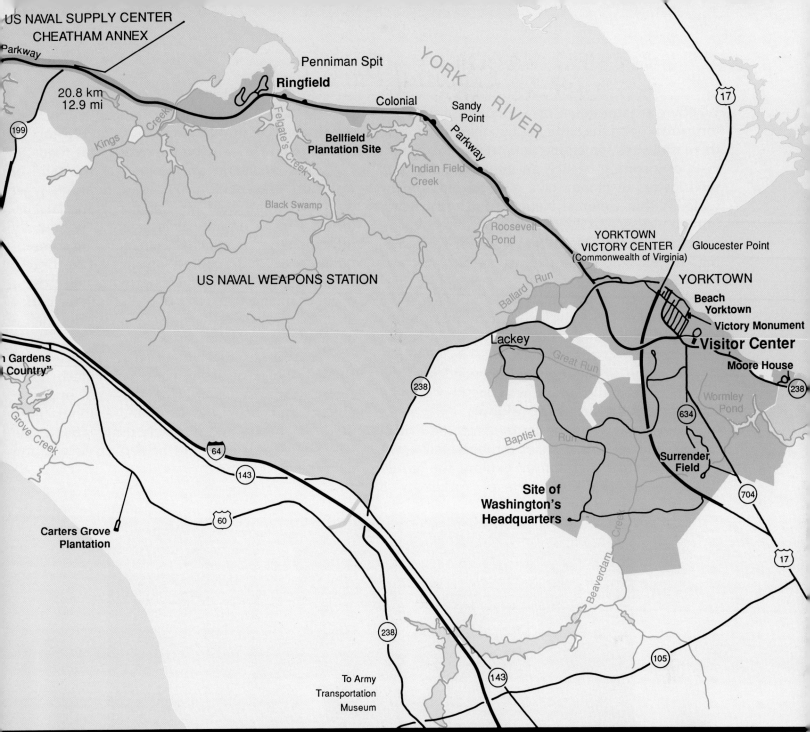

Generally this area is more open and less intimate than Jamestown. Even the wildlife is more often glimpsed at a distance rather than up close. However, at several places deer may be seen in herds of 20 or more, peacefully browsing in early morning or late afternoon.

The Yorktown area conveys a feeling that the land has been used more intensively than at Jamestown. But in contrast, the Yorktown tour drives also reveal a wide variety of natural scenes, from the marsh lands on Beaver Dam Creek to the woodlands above, laced with Civil War earthworks.

Although the park lies in the midst of rapidly increasing urbanization, it is also part of a major complex of military and park installations comprising many thousands of acres. This essentially

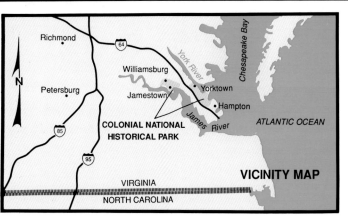

protected expanse provides a wide variety of wildlife habitat and scenic beauty. It is easy to forget that this enclave is actually in the midst of a thriving metropolitan area that presses in on every side.

Colonial Park Today

Whether at Jamestown or Yorktown, in the historic town or on the battlefield, in marsh or forest, there is always something that catches the eye—a vista of inspiring beauty, an intimate glimpse of wildflowers in bloom, or a colorful bird on the wing. Within Colonial National Historical Park, human history and the natural environment combine to offer meaningful and pleasant surroundings for all who come to learn of our past and enjoy the present.

Every year approximately six million visitors tour Colonial. Most enjoy the many interpretive activities, such as the living history participants at the Nelson House, who introduce its owner, a signer of the Declaration of Independence; the glass blowers at the Jamestown Glasshouse; and a tour through the streets of Yorktown.

Some enjoy walking tours along the British Defense Line at Yorktown, or through New Town at Jamestown. Many simply explore the battlefields, or wander the streets of Yorktown as George Washington once did. Others peddle their way by bicycle through the beauty and history of the Colonial Parkway on the park's tour roads.

After 50 years as a pioneer in the field of historical preservation and interpretation, what does the future hold for Colonial National Historical Park? Certainly it is facing a potentially difficult period in which the surrounding communities are expanding rapidly from a quasi-rural to an urban environment. This growth will pose a major challenge to the task of preserving the park's feeling of the past in the midst of drastically changing land use and landscapes.

There is also much that remains to be learned about the history of the park, particularly 17th-century Virginia history. Here is a prime opportunity to look back and learn more about those hardy, vigorous, and intensely pragmatic people who settled this area and helped carve a nation out of the wilderness.

RUSS FINLEY

George Washington, while campaigning, preferred his tents to more permanent structures. They were pitched here where the French and American camps met.

Books in the Story Behind the Scenery series: Acadia, Alcatraz Island, Arches, Biscayne, Blue Ridge Parkway, Bryce Canyon, Canyon de Chelly, Canyonlands, Cape Cod, Capitol Reef, Channel Islands, Civil War Parks, Colonial, Crater Lake, Death Valley, Denali, Devils Tower, Dinosaur, Everglades, Fort Clatsop, Gettysburg, Glacier, Glen Canyon-Lake Powell, Grand Canyon, Grand Canyon-North Rim, Grand Teton, Great Basin, Great Smoky Mountains, Haleakala, Hawaii Volcanoes, Independence, Lake Mead-Hoover Dam, Lassen Volcanic, Lincoln Parks, Mammoth Cave, Mount Rainier, Mount Rushmore, Mount St. Helens, National Park Service, National Seashores, North Cascades, Olympic, Petrified Forest, Redwood, Rocky Mountain, Scotty's Castle, Sequoia & Kings Canyon, Shenandoah, Statue of Liberty, Theodore Roosevelt, Virgin Islands, Yellowstone, Yosemite, Zion.
NEW: in pictures—The Continuing Story: Bryce Canyon, Death Valley, Everglades, Glen Canyon-Lake Powell, Grand Canyon, Mount Rainier, Mount St. Helens, Petrified Forest, Sequoia & Kings Canyon, Yellowstone, Yosemite, Zion.

Published by KC Publications • Box 14429 • Las Vegas, NV 89114

Inside back cover: John Smith's statue faces the sunset on the James River perhaps as Smith did himself almost 400 years ago. Photo by Mae Scanlan.

Back cover: The Church Tower is all that remains above ground to symbolize England's dream for a colonial empire. Photo by Ed Cooper.

Printed by Dong-A Printing and Publishing, Seoul, Korea
Color Separations by Kedia/Kwangyangsa Co., Ltd.